My Book of Grief and Loss

and Loss

A Journal

My Book of Grief and Loss

And Loss

A Journal

Written, illustrated, and mourned over

By _____

Designed and compiled by Judy Shafarman

New Vision

Publications

Printed by Amazon in the United States of America, United Kingdom, European Union, Canada, India, and Australia.

ISBN 978-0-9913226-9-5

Dedicated to the memory of

_____

Introduction

Grieving takes time and sometimes you need to give yourself over to it. Because when you come out on the other side, it can be beautiful.

These words were spoken by Cosette Bonjour who'd been twice widowed before age 60. I found them in a recent edition of the AARP magazine (the American Association of Retired Persons). Of course you don't have to be a member of the age 50+ AARP to know grief and loss. Children losing grandparents, pets or best friends who move away know the pain of loss (not to mention the excruciating tragedy of mourning parents or siblings.)

Bereavement is universal. Primates, dogs, and many other animals all appear to mourn the loss of a mate or companion. Our task in mourning is not to deny the loss but to "come out on the other side" with renewed gratitude for what we now have in our lives and our added resilience and strength.

I am now an over 50 year old myself and I've cried over the deaths of friends and relatives who died long before reaching age 60. I also was saddened by the death of a grandfather who lived a relatively healthy long life (I only knew one of my other grandparents and not on such a close level). I think often of the losses of various people throughout my life and I present this journal writing book to you so you can remember the people you loved who are no longer alive.

Even though when we think of bereavement we tend to think of people dying, my personal truth is that some of my biggest mourning challenges have come from changes of circumstances in my life including ends to romantic relationships (I'll respectfully spare you those details) and moving to a new place. Since reaching the age of majority, I've gone through 6 major geographical moves and various minor moves. Each one leaves a part of me and preserves some strong memories. My adult life in major segments until now has been: university, Peace Corps volunteer, graduate school, and then 3 different small cities until arriving in the one I live in today.

The most recent transition was the hardest for me, much harder than leaving the United States to become the expatriate that I am today. When I married my second husband in 2004, I moved from Jerusalem to live on the Mediterranean coast in Netanya, Israel a mere 60 miles northwest. It should have been a joyous time with the spark of love and excitement. Instead I was in deep grief for a few years. I left my comfortable professional position after a short challenging effort at commuting to my teaching work at the Hebrew University of Jerusalem. I'd left behind some close friendships, which have gradually mellowed into the phone, facebook, and infrequent visit connections I retain today. I'd left behind a whole lifestyle of living among many

American immigrants and other English speakers along with a very active social and cultural life.

There I was over 40 and starting anew to make friendships and build my life while my new husband already had his work and personal connections neatly in place. I mourned and mourned and didn't recognize that period as one of mourning only as a not smooth adjustment to a new marriage.

You've most likely moved a time or two in your adult life and can understand that it can feel like drifting around in a sailboat with no wind for a while as you scout out ways to develop your weekly routine, build relationships and find your purpose.

About three years after that last transition, I saw an advertisement in a local magazine for English speakers to take a course to become a bereavement and loss counselor. This was exactly what I needed as I understood that grief was still affecting my enjoyment of my new home. In a group of about 17 including our trainers, I undertook the course and obligation to give back as a bereavement counselor. And so this teacher became a student again and gradually felt a lot of healing. Our group became quite intimate and included parents who'd lost children and older adults who had dealt with their spouses' or parents' declines and deaths. I faced my pains and grew with this group. In the meanwhile in the last few years, life continued and I've known other losses of dear caring people of my generation and younger.

The tools we gain and wisdom we acquire with wrinkles and passing years must stay at the ready and for me, journal-writing is of constant utility as I reconcile losses or surmount obstacles while rodenting through life's maze. Today I live quite happily with enormous appreciation for my mild climate and beautiful sea views and of course new friendships and my new family with my husband of some 10 years and our son.

As a part-time professional bereavement counselor and not incidentally, a trained life coach, I've learned that I needed to name my pain and rise above it. In the part of the world where I live, the term, post-traumatic stress disorder, is bandied about with great frequency as so many families have lost a member or seen one crippled psychologically or physically. But one of my dear old New Jersey high school friends is the one who uses that term most often to describe her pain at losing the foster kids she'd hoped to adopt. Just wearing the label, PTSD, is not rising above the ache.

Keeping a journal with sacred ritual and quiet time also might not be enough to rise above the grief. Yes, we need time and voice to feel and process the grief, but we also have to spiral up in our writing and re-telling process. In other words, it's not enough to say "I was the victim of this great pain and here now is my miserable tale of it." We have to come to terms, take the loss and become transformed and healed by it. There needs to be some growth and acceptance so that we don't become embittered and stuck in the recycling of the story.

Memoirs, art, songs, films, and poetry have come out the grieving process for some who could express themselves creatively. One such work is a book called, *The Blessing of a Broken Heart* written by an American immigrant to Israel whose 13 year old son was murdered by an Arab terrorist.

The beautifully conceived title asks without asking, what is the blessing from this great pain? It implies that there is a blessing and that the mourner will understand it with time. Nevertheless we can feel the mother's tears over the pages if we choose to read her story. After writing this book, Sherri Mandell and her husband created a foundation in their son's memory to assist bereaved family members following terrorist attacks. Their work continues to aid many hundreds of victims's family members and the organization's fundraising efforts include activities that their son Koby would have loved: benefit performances by comedians and sponsored nature hikes.

Like the Mandell family, we can also find a small or even professional way to commemorate our loss. I've typically chosen small memorials such as planting a tree or donating to charity and now compiling this book .

I don't have my own shocking story of tragedy to tell like Mrs. Mandell. My most dramatic personal story of loss occurred when I was a girl in elementary school and the pain was felt gradually but frequently over many years. My father somehow decided to leave our family in New Jersey to start his dreamed of new life in California. Following his life change, contacts with his 4 children and even child support payments to my mother were mostly overlooked. I mourned not growing up with a father for well over 2 decades before coming to terms with the story I now tell myself which is one of understanding that biological parents are all created differently with different emotional capabilities. My biological father simply wasn't "cut out" to be a father at all.

Long before I truly acknowledged all the facets to my daughterly anger and grief, I was awed by a college roommate who had divorced parents and a very active on-going relationship with her father. Her guidance along with a strong cathartic cry I had while watching the movie *Kramer vs. Kramer* (1979) gave me an understanding that my bereavement from growing up without a father was utterly rational. I learned that "therapy" and healing can come from social interactions and close friendships as well as film or literature, and of course, journal writing.

Having a journal by my side in high school and university and in my solitude in a small village in West Africa was an anchor and a forum. Angers and lessons learned came out in the journals. As it turned out, I had to experience a lot of learning about the opposite sex and my own sexuality and making my way in the big scary world with little emotional support from either of my parents. Through all those growing years, journals, fantastic women friends and some traditional psychotherapy were invaluable to me. I'm still and always blessed by my journals and special women friends and as the great Stephen Sondheim song goes, "I'm still here."

So, I am a great believer and user of reflective journal writing. I often carry small notebooks to write down ideas along with moods and emotions. My previous books on journal-writing talk more about how I use my journals. My first book explains how regular journaling can cultivate joy and well-being. A journal writer takes a few minutes to sit peacefully and pour words on paper to release them. These words can now be let go if they contain anger, self-pity or pain. By contrast they can be savored and relished if they are full of

gratitude and love. The first book gives you a year of up-
lifting ideas and is so named: **Journal: 365+ writing
prompts, ideas, and quotes to cultivate joy and well-
being.**

The second book in its paperback form is formatted as a
sibling to this one. It's an example of a journal with a quote
alongside a page for writing, scribbling, doodling, sketching
or even pasting in pictures. Since nowadays people want to
walk around with their kindles or tablets, all of my books are
sold digitally and available in all digital formats for I-pod,
smartphone, android, PC, or kindle. I suggest you copy the
quotes and prompts that you like into your spiral or other
bound personal journal, but that's also because quote
collecting has been prominent in my journal writing since
high school.

So even as I was creating **My book of Appreciation: a
journal**, I knew that I wanted a companion volume for those
who wish to open their hearts and feel their pain over the
losses they've experienced in life. Hence you have **My book
of Grief**. In either the paperback which is the whole journal
with space for your writing or the digital form, I offer you a
framework to create your own journal of memories, aches
and gradual some sort of resolution. I arranged the quotes
more or less to put the weepiest toward the beginning and
some words of hope and renewal as the journal goes on but
of course there is no direct elevator to up in talking of the
spirit and overcoming loss in our lives.

The pains and pangs will re-visit you from time to time and
new pains and pangs will appear. Even the great grief writer,

Elisabeth Kübler-Ross who first created the five- stage paradigm of grief—denial and shock, anger, bargaining, depression, acceptance -- knew at the end of her life, that grief was individual and the stage model was not linear. Your process may take months or the rest of your life; you'll never be exactly the same person as before the loss.

Still even Kübler-Ross thought that we could take our mourning or the death of a loved one and find growth and learning from the pain. Journal writing can help us to process not just our emotions but also our fragile growth. In terms of using this or another book, I suggest you wait a few weeks or months after that first "denial" "shock" or "anger" in which words may not be at the fore. The intensity of your feeling may not lend itself to the quiet contemplative gift of journaling.

The power of the pen is mighty; we all know that. No one is checking your spelling or grammar. Just let it fly. You can of course use a keyboard and keep your journal password-protected and private. I favor the pen because it allows doodles and colors and bold hard presses along with whispered light touches. Both researchers and general authors have found that handwriting links to different neural pathways and invites a different sort of expression than keyboard tapping.

Along with many others who have written about journal writing including research psychologists, I am an obvious convert to the therapeutic value of journal writing. In the case of dealing with the feelings arising from losses both sudden and not, the journal has some great advantages. In particular, it's portable, available in the middle of an insomniac's challenged night, non-judgmental and never bored by repetition.

My journals have enabled me to process the losses at young age of dear people in my life who died of illness or accidents. They have come with me in my changes of residence and country. They guided me through my adolescence and the grief of realizing that I didn't have perfect parents who could magically soothe life's challenges.

When fire mostly destroyed my bedroom in January1997, I was aggrieved by the destruction of my journal representing my internal and true self as well as, of course, the physical loss of my clothes and furniture which showed the world my outer layer and represented monetary loss and the discomfort of displacement during the renovation. A new journal that winter contains many words of appreciation for all the kindnesses that were extended to me during the 3 weeks I had to be housed by a caring friend along with the anger over the material losses.

My journal-writing gets to the core of who I am. I am revealed to myself with visions, gratitude and joy but also with angers, pains and losses that come with a life in a society of people, things, and pets.

Use the ideas in this journal freely and randomly. Choose those quotes and prompts that call out to you; skip those pages you want to skip. Add your own quotes and poems on the left-hand page. Start with the writing prompt and go ahead and write for 4-15 minutes or more as a beginning or end to your day or use it during a 4 pm coffee break. I like to write the day of the week, date and time that I write. You might also want to include weather or some other background details for whenever you re-read your writing or if you want to pass your journal onto another grieving family member. Make use of the page with the quote as well as the one opposite it with doodles or pasted in photographs, as you choose. All in all, keep your journaling practice short and confined, you do after all, have a day of other things to do beyond the mournfulness.

Many people report healing and relief from having a trusted journal writing and reading partner. If this appeals to you, I suggest you find someone who has a different loss to grieve so that you each comfort the other in your separate situations rather than finding yourselves like the professional funeral ladies in some cultures who become extremely loud wailers during the procession to draw attention to themselves and the funeral and behave as if to say that no one could suffer more than they. There are many possibilities for locating such a safe partner to share the process of coming to terms with loss. In many large communities social workers or trained counselors conduct bereavement groups. In one such group, you might find a person who can become your writing buddy. If you've identified yourself with any sort of 12-step or other support group you might find a confidante through that fellowship. Or do a serious search on the internet and find someone who lives outside of your community with whom to connect by Skype or telephone 1-4 times a month and read out your private writing.

As a counselor, I would suggest a time frame for this work, say 3 to 5 months. Your memories of the lost past will stay a part of you forever, but the active grief work needs to fade from your daily life patterns. This book contains 101 quotes, poems and prompts. You can use it daily for about 14 weeks if you choose or revisit it several times a week and intersperse it with free-writing or other prompted journal writing. I included more poems in this compilation than in **My Book of Appreciation** because so many mourners have reported feeling consoled by poetry. Write out what's on your heart and in your soul. Maybe you'll create your own poetry, song or other tribute which you can draft out in your journal-writing.

Be loving and kind to your writing and mourning self. Often this period will bring to mind additional losses and aches from other times in your life even from many years prior or early childhood. Allow yourself to swim with the waves of the feelings and not drown. The journal can be hugely helpful for riding the tide and expressing the emotions.

We who live in a modern world know too well from people both near and far as well as memoirs, movies and tabloid articles, that it's enormously tempting to ignore feelings and get lost in abuse of alcohol, food addictions, narcotics, computer games, gambling excess, internet addiction, workaholism, etc. Releasing yourself through journal-writing might be a small help to avoid the downward slope of "soft" or worse addictions in addition to acrimony and angst. In concert, many mourners find benefit from professional counseling or organized bereavement groups. Don't discount the power of professional therapy if you start falling into a compulsive self-destructive well. Psychotherapists and professional counselors save lives along with psychiatrists who can prescribe anti-depressants. Anti-anxiety medications, or sleeping pills if such are warranted.

When I was a young girl and I saw the original TV movie of *Brian's Song* about the death from cancer of a football player, I hadn't had any personal contact with cancer patients and I was embarrassed to let my older brothers see the tears in my eyes. It was my first instance of being moved to tears from a movie. I've been a fan of the cathartic cry type of movie, song or poem ever since when it speaks to my mood. For me movies and literature can do a world of good in accepting the human condition.

There are some beautiful meaningful titles on works about death and loss in addition to Sherri Mandell's. What title would you write for this period in your life? Here's a small sample of some painful but meaningful article, book, and movie titles that appeal to me. (I'm not necessarily endorsing any of the works; I like the titles).

- It's My Crisis and I'll Cry If I Need to
- A New Normal
- Life after Loss
- Ordinary People
- Good Grief
- Healing the Greatest Hurt
- The Work of Mourning
- The Courage to Grieve
- A Grief Observed
- I wasn't ready to say goodbye

Whoever or whatever you have lost and mourn in this book of grief, it is not gone as long as you survive with your memories and stories. After my grandfather died more than two decades ago, I was advised to remember him well so that I could choose to tell of his life to descendants of mine. And so stories are passed forward.

As a consequence of the few minutes you take in private journaling, the people around you who care about you may see you as more calm and accepting as you put your distress silently on paper rather than excessively re-playing the pain for them.

May you be comforted by your journal writing, by your surviving loved ones and all that you find to appreciate and grow with and learn from in the world you inhabit.

With love and blessings,

Judy Shafarman

P.S. I am so jazzed about the healing and growth potential of journal writing, I'd like to give you an extra free e-book of sparks for writing and cultivating joy. Simply write to me at judy@judyshafarman.net and at the same time write with any ideas or comments you have.

To weep is to make less the depth of grief.

William Shakespeare, *Henry VI, Part II*

Today's date   /   /

1..Today it is okay to weep, bawl, cry and shed tears.

_____

_____

_____

_____

_____

_____

_____

_____

_____

_____

_____

_____

_____

_____

_____

_____

_____

_____

_____

_____

Grief is not a disorder, a disease or a sign of weakness. It is an emotional, physical and spiritual necessity, the price you pay for love. The only cure for grief is to grieve.
Earl Grollman

2. What does the word, "grief" mean to me?

_/_   _/_

_____

_____

_____

_____

_____

_____

_____

_____

_____

_____

_____

_____

_____

_____

_____

_____

_____

_____

_____

A grief without a pang, void, dark and drear,

A drowsy, stifled, unimpassioned grief,

Which finds no natural outlet or relief,

In word, or sigh, or tear.

Samuel Taylor Coleridge

3. How can I live in this darkness? ___/___/___

_____
_____
_____
_____
_____
_____
_____
_____
_____
_____
_____
_____
_____
_____
_____
_____
_____
_____
_____
_____
_____
_____
_____
_____
_____
_____

There is a sacredness in tears

They are not the mark of weakness,

but of power.

They speak more eloquently

than 10,000 tongues.

They are the messengers

of overwhelming grief,

of deep contrition,

and of unspeakable love.

Washington Irving

4. Maybe there are no words for the love I felt

Grief is a wound that needs attention in order to heal. To work through and complete grief means to face our feelings openly and honestly, to express or release our feelings fully, and to tolerate and accept our feelings for however long it takes the wound to heal.

Judy Tatelbaum

5. Feeling

_____
_____
_____
_____
_____
_____
_____
_____
_____
_____
_____
_____
_____
_____
_____
_____
_____
_____
_____
_____
_____
_____
_____
_____

Will there really be a morning?

Is there such a thing as day?

Could I see it from the mountains

If I were as tall as they?

Has it feet like water lilies?

Has it feathers like a bird?

Is it brought from famous countries

Of which I have never heard?

Oh, some scholar! Oh, some sailor!

Oh, some wise man from the skies?

Please to tell a little pilgrim

Where the place called morning lies.

Emily Dickinson

6. I can feel a new day starting.   / /

_____

_____

_____

_____

_____

_____

_____

_____

_____

_____

_____

_____

_____

_____

_____

_____

_____

_____

_____

_____

_____

Unless you have been very, very lucky, you have undoubtedly experienced events in your life that have made you cry. So unless you have been very, very lucky, you know that a good, long session of weeping can often make you feel better, even if your circumstances have not changed one bit.

Lemony Snicket, a. k a. writer, Daniel Handler

7. Young children are so good at crying and releasing their emotions. Maybe I need to take a page from their books.

/ /

_____

_____

_____

_____

_____

_____

_____

_____

_____

_____

_____

_____

_____

_____

_____

_____

_____

_____

Walking with a friend in the dark is better than walking alone in the light.

Helen Keller

8. I am not alone in my grief. I / /
appreciate the comfort of:

_____

_____

_____

_____

_____

_____

_____

_____

_____

_____

_____

_____

_____

_____

_____

_____

_____

_____

_____

While grief is fresh, every attempt to divert only irritates. You must wait till it be digested, and then amusement will dissipate the remains of it.

Samuel Johnson

9. I am not at all ready to divert my grief, but I can start to digest it.

/ /

_____
_____
_____
_____
_____
_____
_____
_____
_____
_____
_____
_____
_____
_____
_____
_____
_____
_____
_____

I lit a candle tonight, in honor of you.

Remembering your life, and all the times we'd been through.

Such a small little light the candle made until I realized how much darkness it lit on the way.

All the tears I've cried in all my grief and pain what a garden they grew; watered with human rain.

I sometimes can't see beyond the moment, in hopeless despair.

But then your memory sustains me, in heartaches' repair.

I can't wait for the tomorrow, when my sorrows ease.

Until then, I'll light this candle, and let my memories run free.

Source unknown

10. The light of a candle on my pain: / /

Happiness is beneficial for the body, but it is grief that develops the powers of the mind.

Marcel Proust

11. Somehow this grief may really develop and shape my mind.

_____ / _____ / _____

_____
_____
_____
_____
_____
_____
_____
_____
_____
_____
_____
_____
_____
_____
_____
_____
_____
_____
_____
_____
_____

The darker the night, the brighter
the stars,
The deeper the grief, the closer is
God!
Fyodor Dostoyevsky

12. Where now is God or my higher power?

Tears are words
that need to be written.

Paulo Coelho

13. The words that need to be written: / /

_____

_____

_____

_____

_____

_____

_____

_____

_____

_____

_____

_____

_____

_____

_____

_____

_____

_____

_____

_____

_____

Grief is a normal and natural response to loss. It is originally an unlearned feeling process. Keeping grief inside increases your pain.

Ann Grant

14. Thoughts on my grief:

/ /

_____
_____
_____
_____
_____
_____
_____
_____
_____
_____
_____
_____
_____
_____
_____
_____
_____
_____
_____
_____
_____
_____
_____

Death leaves a heartache no one can heal.
Love leaves a memory no one can steal.

Found on a gravestone somewhere in Ireland

15. An epitaph:

_____

_____

_____

_____

_____

_____

_____

_____

_____

_____

_____

_____

_____

_____

_____

_____

_____

_____

_____

_____

_____

_____

Guilt is perhaps the most painful companion to death.
Elisabeth Kübler-Ross

16. I absolve myself from all guilt surrounding my loss. But before I release it, I can briefly write out what I would have to feel guilty about if I wanted to dwell in feeling miserable.

_____

_____

_____

_____

_____

_____

_____

_____

_____

_____

_____

_____

_____

_____

_____

_____

_____

_____

Do Not Stand at My Grave and Weep
Do not stand at my grave and weep,
I am not there, I do not sleep.
I am in a thousand winds that blow,
I am the softly falling snow.
I am the gentle showers of rain,
I am the fields of ripening grain.
I am in the morning hush,
I am in the graceful rush
Of beautiful birds in circling flight,
I am the star shine of the night.
I am in the flowers that bloom,
I am in a quiet room.
I am in the birds that sing,
I am in each lovely thing.
Do not stand at my grave and cry,
I am not there. I do not die.

Mary Elizabeth Frye

17. How that which I lost is still part of my life.

    / /

_____

_____

_____

_____

_____

_____

_____

_____

_____

_____

_____

_____

_____

_____

_____

_____

_____

_____

_____

_____

Someday you're gonna look back on this moment of your life as such a sweet time of grieving. You'll see that you were in mourning and your heart was broken, but your life was changing...

Elizabeth Gilbert

18. What might be sweet about my grieving? / /

Give sorrow words; the grief that does not speak knits up the over wrought heart and bids it break.

William Shakespeare, *MacBeth*

19. Words for my sorrow.

grief is a house
where the chairs
have forgotten how to hold us
the mirrors how to reflect us
the walls how to contain us

grief is a house that disappears
each time someone knocks at the door
or rings the bell
a house that blows into the air
at the slightest gust
that buries itself deep in the ground
while everyone is sleeping

grief is a house where no one can protect
you
where the younger sister
will grow older than the older one
where the doors
no longer let you in
or out

Jandy Nelson

20. How am I caught in the house of grief and where is the door out?

_____

_____

_____

_____

_____

_____

_____

_____

_____

_____

_____

_____

_____

_____

_____

_____

_____

_____

_____

We were promised sufferings. They were part of the program. We were even told, 'Blessed are they that mourn,' and I accept it. I've got nothing that I hadn't bargained for. Of course it is different when the thing happens to oneself, not to others, and in reality, not imagination.

C. S. Lewis

21. Yes, yes, yes, I knew life entailed loss. But how long must I suffer?

_____
_____
_____
_____
_____
_____
_____
_____
_____
_____
_____
_____
_____
_____
_____
_____
_____
_____
_____
_____

To whom could I put this question
(with any hope of an answer)?
Does being able to live without
someone you loved mean you
loved her less than you thought...?

Roland Barthes

22. I am thankful for the love I felt.   / /

Self-pity in its early stages is as snug as a feather mattress.

Only when it hardens does it become uncomfortable.

Maya Angelou

23. When is it okay for me to feel sorry for myself and when not?

_/ /_

You are not enclosed within your bodies, nor confined to houses or fields. That which is you dwells above the mountain and roves with the wind....

Kahlil Gibran

24. A tribute to you:

/ /

We look before and after,
And pine for what is not;
Our sincerest laughter
With some pain is fraught;
Our sweetest songs are those that tell
Of saddest thought.

Percy Bysshe Shelley

25. A sad song

_____

_____

_____

_____

_____

_____

_____

_____

_____

_____

_____

_____

_____

_____

_____

_____

_____

_____

_____

_____

_____

_____

_____

When someone you love becomes a memory,

the memory becomes a treasure.

Source unknown

26. A page for expressing the
bittersweet beauty and pain.

/ /

The grief within me has its own heartbeat.

It has its own life, its own song.

Part of me wants to resist the rhythms of my grief, yet as I surrender to the song, I learn to listen deep within myself

Alan Wolfelt

27. What life, what heartbeat does my grief have?

_____

_____

_____

_____

_____

_____

_____

_____

_____

_____

_____

_____

_____

_____

_____

_____

_____

_____

_____

_____

_____

_____

_____

When a loss hits us, we have not only the particular loss to mourn but also the shattered beliefs and assumptions of what life should be. These life beliefs must be mourned separately. Sometimes we must grieve for them first. We can't grieve the loss if we are in the midst of "It's not supposed to happen this way" . . . We intellectually know that bad things happen – but to other people, not us, and certainly not in the world we assumed we were living in . .

Elisabeth Kübler-Ross

28. Yes, I used to think such loss happened to other people not to me. What assumptions and beliefs have now been shattered?

_____

_____

_____

_____

_____

_____

_____

_____

_____

_____

_____

_____

_____

_____

_____

_____

_____

Those we love and lose are always connected by heartstrings into infinity.

Terri Guillemets

29. "Rest in Peace" -- Where is my peace?

/ /

_____

_____

_____

_____

_____

_____

_____

_____

_____

_____

_____

_____

_____

_____

_____

_____

_____

_____

_____

_____

_____

With what a deep devotedness of woe
I wept thy absence - o'er and o'er again
Thinking of thee, still thee, till thought grew pain,
And memory, like a drop that, night and day,
Falls cold and ceaseless, wore my heart away!

Thomas Moore

30. I let go of anger. I let go of woe. I
feel my heart.

_____ / _ /

_____

_____

_____

_____

_____

_____

_____

_____

_____

_____

_____

_____

_____

_____

_____

_____

_____

_____

_____

Music, when soft voices die,
Vibrates in the memory,
Odours, when sweet violets sicken,
Live within the sense they quicken.

Rose leaves, when the rose is dead,
Are heaped for the beloved's bed;
And so thy thoughts, when thou art gone,
Love itself shall slumber on.

Percy Bysshe Shelley

31. My mournful music.

Absence is a house so vast that
inside you will pass through its walls
and hang pictures on the air.

Pablo Neruda

32. How does the absence hang in the air as I write today?

_____
_____
_____
_____
_____
_____
_____
_____
_____
_____
_____
_____
_____
_____
_____
_____
_____
_____

"The best thing for being sad," replied Merlyn, beginning to puff and blow, "is to learn something. That is the only thing that never fails. You may grow old and trembling in your anatomies, you may lie awake at night listening to the disorder in your veins, you may miss your only love, you may see the world about you devastated by evil lunatics, or know your honour trampled in the sewer of baser minds. There is only one thing for it then—to learn.."

Advice to young King Arthur

from T. H. White, *The Once and Future King*

33. What advice can my older, wiser self give to my sad self today?

_____

_____

_____

_____

_____

_____

_____

_____

_____

_____

_____

_____

_____

_____

_____

_____

_____

_____

_____

Mourning has its place
but also its limits.

Joan Didion

34. How many minutes shall I give over to mourning today?

_____

_____

_____

_____

_____

_____

_____

_____

_____

_____

_____

_____

_____

_____

_____

_____

_____

_____

_____

_____

In sorrow we must go, but not in despair. Behold! we are not bound forever to the circles of the world, and beyond them is more than memory.

J.R.R. Tolkien

35. More than memory. Circles and cycles of the world.

Life is eternal, and love is immortal,
and death is only a horizon;
and a horizon is nothing save the limit
of our sight.
Rossiter Worthington Raymond

36. On the horizon

_____

_____

_____

_____

_____

_____

_____

_____

_____

_____

_____

_____

_____

_____

_____

_____

_____

_____

_____

_____

_____

_____

Sorrow makes us all children again - destroys all differences of intellect.

The wisest know nothing.

Ralph Waldo Emerson

37. I can allow myself to be like a child in my bereavement

/ /

_____
_____
_____
_____
_____
_____
_____
_____
_____
_____
_____
_____
_____
_____
_____
_____
_____
_____
_____
_____

Hold on to what is good even if it is a handful of earth.

Hold on to what you believe even if it is a tree which stands by itself.

Hold on to what you must do even if it is a long way from here.

Hold on to life even when it is easier letting go.

Hold on to my hand even when I have gone away from you.

A Native American blessing

38. A hand, a lifeline. I learned from you:

_____

_____

_____

_____

_____

_____

_____

_____

_____

_____

_____

_____

_____

_____

_____

_____

_____

_____

Grieving allows us to heal, to remember with love rather than pain. It is a sorting process. One by one you let go of the things that are gone and you mourn for them. One by one you take hold of the things that have become a part of who you are and build again.

Rachel Naomi Remen

39. One by one

_____

_____

_____

_____

_____

_____

_____

_____

_____

_____

_____

_____

_____

_____

_____

_____

_____

_____

_____

_____

_____

_____

_____

The Rainy Day

The day is cold, and dark, and dreary;
It rains and the wind is never weary;
The vine still clings to the mouldering wall,
But at every gust the dead leaves fall,
    And the day is dark and dreary.

My life is cold, and dark and dreary;
It rains, and the wind is never weary.
My thoughts still cling to the mouldering past,
But the hopes of youth fall thick in the blast,
    And the days are dark and dreary.

Be still, sad heart! And cease repining;
Behind the clouds is the sun still shining;
Thy fate is the common fate of all,
Into each life some rain must fall,
    Some days must be dark and dreary.

Henry Wadsworth Longfellow

40. "Into each life some rain must fall,
Some days must be dark and dreary."
How might I mourn my youth and how
can I gaze upon and feel the falling
rain?

_____

_____

_____

_____

_____

_____

_____

_____

_____

_____

_____

_____

_____

_____

_____

_____

_____

_____

Question me now about all other matters, but do not ask who I am, for fear you may increase in my heart its burden of sorrow as I think back. I am very full of grief, and I should not sit in the house of somebody else with my lamentation and wailing. It is not good to go on mourning forever.

Homer, The Odyssey

41. And now a mundane, "normal" journal entry about all other matters

/ /

_____

_____

_____

_____

_____

_____

_____

_____

_____

_____

_____

_____

_____

_____

_____

_____

_____

_____

_____

_____

_____

Although it's difficult today to see
beyond the sorrow,
May looking back in memory help
comfort you tomorrow.

Source Unknown

42. A terrific memory:

_____

_____

_____

_____

_____

_____

_____

_____

_____

_____

_____

_____

_____

_____

_____

_____

_____

_____

_____

Hope is important because it can make the present moment less difficult to bear. If we believe that tomorrow will be better, we can bear a hardship today.

Thich Nhat Hanh

43. How much more do I want to use words like hardship, suffering and despair?

_____

_____

_____

_____

_____

_____

_____

_____

_____

_____

_____

_____

_____

_____

_____

_____

_____

_____

_____

_____

_____

If tears could build a stairway,
And memories a lane,
I'd walk right up to Heaven
And bring you home again.
Source Unknown

44. A page for memories

/ /

The span between life and death can be as quick and sudden as a puff of wind that blows out a candle. But the candle does not suffer after darkness comes. It is the person left in the dark room who gropes and stumbles.

Helen Duke Fike

45. Candle or darkness?

_____
_____
_____
_____
_____
_____
_____
_____
_____
_____
_____
_____
_____
_____
_____
_____
_____
_____
_____
_____
_____
_____
_____
_____

Alone

I am alone, in spite of love,

In spite of all I take and give—

In spite of all your tenderness,

Sometimes I am not glad to live.

I am alone, as though I stood

On the highest peak of the tired gray world,

About me only swirling snow,

Above me, endless space unfurled;

With earth hidden and heaven hidden,

To keep me from the peace of those

Who are not lonely, having died.

Sara Teasdale

46. Solo, alone, in solitude I write / /

I walked a mile with Pleasure.

She chattered all the way,

But left me none the wiser

For all she had to say.

I walked a mile with Sorrow,

And ne'er a word said she;

But oh, the things

I learned from her

When Sorrow walked with me!

Robert Browning

47. What does silent Sorrow teach me?   / /

_____

_____

_____

_____

_____

_____

_____

_____

_____

_____

_____

_____

_____

_____

_____

_____

_____

_____

_____

_____

_____

_____

_____

Upon being asked, why I am not writing -

Too much gone wrong-

No muse, no song.

Barry Tebb

48. No muse, a doodle

/   /

Gain from your present loss may be obtained today.

No man may reckon on tomorrow.

Fruit, when ripe, not gathered, will decay.

The soil which showers soften, soon becomes dry.

Perhaps you think this weeping will be life-long--joys will be buried in this grave--the sun of earthly happiness is set.

But the darkest night will have a dawn.

Time's hand has art to efface the writing of an iron pen, and to heal the scars which sorrow has infixed.

To customary employ you will return; and as you have been, so you may be again.

Unless you come forth wholly changed, you will remain more hopelessly the same.

The furnace, which refines the ore, hardens the flint.

The sun, which melts the snow, converts the clay to stone.

Your sorrow brings a blessing or a curse.

The warmth which opens flowers, revives the frost-bound adder.

Henry Law (part of a sermon from the 19th century)

49. How do I react when someone hints that "time heals"?

_____

_____

_____

_____

_____

_____

_____

_____

_____

_____

_____

_____

_____

_____

_____

_____

_____

_____

_____

_____

Even if you've lost the love of your life, you've not been cheated by life no matter how tragic the circumstances, but we cheat life if we close our hearts after we've lost someone.

Geoff Warburton

50. How can I stop cheating life? / /

Real grief is not healed by time.
If time does anything, it deepens our grief.
The longer we live, the more fully we become aware of
who she was for us,
and the more intimately we experience what her love
meant to us.
Real, deep love is, as you know, very unobtrusive,
seemingly easy and obvious, and so present that we
take it for granted.
Therefore, it is only in retrospect—or better, in
memory—
that we fully realize its power and depth.
Yes, indeed, love often makes itself visible in pain.

Henri Nouwen

51. My love for you can endure the passing of time and your passing from life

/   /

Tears, idle tears, I know not what they mean,
Tears from the depths of some devine despair
Rise in the heart, and gather to the eyes,
In looking on the happy autumn fields,
And thinking of the days that are no more.

Alfred Lord Tennyson

52.   How old I feel

_____

_____

_____

_____

_____

_____

_____

_____

_____

_____

_____

_____

_____

_____

_____

_____

_____

_____

_____

_____

_____

_____

You don't get over it, you just get through it.

You don't get by it, because you can't get around it.

It doesn't 'get better.'

It just gets different.

Everyday grief puts on a new face. -

Wendy Feireis

53. A face for my grief

/ /

We must embrace pain and burn it as fuel for our journey.

Kenji Miyazawa

54. Fuel for my journey

Courage is being afraid and going on the journey anyhow.

John Wayne

55. How much John Wayne swagger and courage can I muster for today? / /

_____

_____

_____

_____

_____

_____

_____

_____

_____

_____

_____

_____

_____

_____

_____

_____

_____

_____

_____

Loss alone is but the wounding of a heart;

it is memory that makes it our ruin.

Brian Ruckley

56. What memories can I put in my head when sleep is trying to overtake me?

_____
_____
_____
_____
_____
_____
_____
_____
_____
_____
_____
_____
_____
_____
_____
_____
_____
_____
_____

I measure every Grief I meet
With narrow, probing, eyes—
I wonder if It weighs like Mine—
Or has an Easier size.

I wonder if They bore it long—
Or did it just begin—
I could not tell the Date of Mine—
It feels so old a pain—

I wonder if it hurts to live—
And if They have to try —
And whether—could They choose between—
It would not be—to die—

I note that Some—gone patient long—
At length, renew their smile—
An imitation of a Light
That has so little Oil—

I wonder if when Years have piled—
Some Thousands—on the Harm—
That hurt them early—such a lapse
Could give them any Balm—

Or would they go on aching still
Through Centuries of Nerve–
Enlightened to a larger Pain–
In Contrast with the Love –

The Grieved –are many –I am told –
There is the various Cause –
Death – is but one –and comes but once –
And only nails the eyes –

There's Grief of Want – and grief of Cold –
A sort they call "Despair" –
There's Banishment from native Eyes –
In sight of Native Air –

And though I may not guess the kind –
Correctly – yet to me
A piercing Comfort it affords
In passing Calvary –

To note the fashions – of the Cross–
And how they're mostly worn –
Still fascinated to presume
That Some – are like my own –

Emily Dickinson

57. How and when do "I measure every grief I meet?" / /

_____

_____

_____

_____

_____

_____

_____

_____

_____

_____

_____

_____

_____

_____

_____

_____

_____

_____

_____

_____

_____

And can it be that in a world so full and busy the loss of one creature makes a void so wide and deep that nothing but the width and depth of eternity can fill it up!

Charles Dickens

58. I simply miss you because   / /

_____

_____

_____

_____

_____

_____

_____

_____

_____

_____

_____

_____

_____

_____

_____

_____

_____

_____

_____

We can endure much more than we think we can; all human experience testifies to that. All we need to do is learn not to be afraid of pain. Grit your teeth and let it hurt. Don't deny it, don't be overwhelmed by it. It will not last forever. One day, the pain will be gone and you will still be there.

Harold Kushner

59. Still here and thinking about ... / /

_____

_____

_____

_____

_____

_____

_____

_____

_____

_____

_____

_____

_____

_____

_____

_____

_____

_____

_____

_____

_____

_____

The family exists for many reasons, but its most basic function may be to draw together after a member dies.

Stephen King

60. How have family members aided me through this time? / /

_____

_____

_____

_____

_____

_____

_____

_____

_____

_____

_____

_____

_____

_____

_____

_____

_____

_____

_____

_____

No one ever told me that grief felt so much like fear.

C.S. Lewis

61. Okay self, what do you fear?

_____

_____

_____

_____

_____

_____

_____

_____

_____

_____

_____

_____

_____

_____

_____

_____

_____

_____

_____

_____

_____

The world is full of suffering. It is also full of the overcoming of it.

Helen Keller

62. How much longer must I still suffer this pain?

_____

_____

_____

_____

_____

_____

_____

_____

_____

_____

_____

_____

_____

_____

_____

_____

_____

_____

_____

_____

Consolation springs from sources deeper far than deepest suffering.

William Wordsworth

63. Where inside of my deepest depths can I find some consolation?

/ /

Hope never abandons you.
You abandon hope.

George Weinberg

64. Dear Hope, I want to say to you

/ /

_____

_____

_____

_____

_____

_____

_____

_____

_____

_____

_____

_____

_____

_____

_____

_____

_____

_____

_____

_____

_____

_____

_____

_____

_____

What we have once enjoyed deeply we can never lose. All that we love deeply becomes a part of us.

Helen Keller

65. How you became a part of me

_____

_____

_____

_____

_____

_____

_____

_____

_____

_____

_____

_____

_____

_____

_____

_____

_____

_____

_____

_____

_____

Life's under no obligation to give us what we expect.

Margaret Mitchell

66. What I expected. How frivolous are expectations.

    /   /

Oh heart, if one should say to you that the soul perishes like the body, answer that the flower withers, but the seed remains.

Kahlil Gibran

67. Seeds you planted

Grief is a process,
not a state.
Anne Grant

68. Because I am undergoing this difficult daily process of life, I know that I am human and not a rock.

/ /

_____
_____
_____
_____
_____
_____
_____
_____
_____
_____
_____
_____
_____
_____
_____
_____
_____
_____

There is no grief like the grief that does not speak.

Henry Wordsworth

69. Words to speak about my grief   /   /

I can be changed by what happens to me, but I refuse to be reduced by it.

Maya Angelou

70. How might I be changed from what I've been through in this grief?

_/ /_

_____

_____

_____

_____

_____

_____

_____

_____

_____

_____

_____

_____

_____

_____

_____

_____

_____

_____

_____

_____

In this sad world of ours sorrow comes to all and it often comes with bitter agony. Perfect relief is not possible except with time. You cannot now believe that you will ever feel better. But this is not true. You are sure to be happy again. Knowing this, truly believing it will make you less miserable now. I have had enough experience to make this statement.

Abraham Lincoln

71. What I can believe today:

/ /

_____

_____

_____

_____

_____

_____

_____

_____

_____

_____

_____

_____

_____

_____

_____

_____

_____

_____

_____

_____

_____

When I come to the end of the road
And the sun has set for me
I want no rites in a gloom filled room
Why cry for a soul set free?

Miss me a little, but not for long
And not with your head bowed low
Remember the love that once we shared
Miss me, but let me go.

For this is a journey we all must take
And each must go alone.
It's all part of the master plan
A step on the road to home.

When you are lonely and sick at heart
Go to the friends we know.
Laugh at all the things we used to do
Miss me, but let me go.

Christina Rossetti

72. Today as I write, I am missing   / /

Life seems more sweet that thou didst live,

And men more true that thou wert one;

Nothing is lost that thou didst give,

Nothing destroyed that thou hast done.

Anne Brontë

73. What you gave to the world— your legacy

/ /

_____

_____

_____

_____

_____

_____

_____

_____

_____

_____

_____

_____

_____

_____

_____

_____

_____

_____

_____

_____

_____

_____

In everyone's life, at some time, our inner fire goes out. It is then burst into flame by an encounter with another human being. We should all be thankful for those people who rekindle the inner spirit.

Albert Schweitzer

74. I bless my memory of the person I dedicated this book to who kindled my inner spirit. Who might rekindle some flame for me?

_____

_____

_____

_____

_____

_____

_____

_____

_____

_____

_____

_____

_____

_____

_____

_____

_____

_____

We carry the dead with us only until we die too, and then it is we who are borne along for a little while, and then our bearers in their turn drop, and so on into the unimaginable generations.

John Banville

75. I will not forget my loss. It becomes a part of my self-definition.

/ /

_____
_____
_____
_____
_____
_____
_____
_____
_____
_____
_____
_____
_____
_____
_____
_____
_____
_____
_____
_____
_____
_____

He spake well who said that graves are the footprints of angels.

Henry Wadsworth Longfellow

76. How have "angels" been speaking or signaling to me?

_____

_____

_____

_____

_____

_____

_____

_____

_____

_____

_____

_____

_____

_____

_____

_____

_____

_____

_____

Any appeal to fairness was absurd. I was led by my fellow suffers, those I loved and those who had also endured irredeemable losses, to find reasons to go on.

Like all who mourn I learned an abiding hatred for the word, "closure," with its comforting implications that grief is a time-limited process from which we will all recover. The idea that I could reach a point when I would no longer miss my children was obscene to me and I dismissed it. I had to accept the reality that I would never be the same person, that some part of my heart, perhaps the best part, had been cut out and buried with my sons. What was left? Now *there* was a question worth contemplating.

Gordon Livingston who lost a son to suicide and one to leukemia within 13 months.

77. What does my heart look and feel like now after the loss?

_____/_____/_____

_____

_____

_____

_____

_____

_____

_____

_____

_____

_____

_____

_____

_____

_____

_____

_____

_____

_____

_____

_____

_____

_____

We carry the dead with us only until we die too, and then it is we who are borne along for a little while, and then our bearers in their turn drop, and so on into the unimaginable generations.

John Banville

78. I will not forget my loss. It becomes a part of my self-definition.

/ /

_____

_____

_____

_____

_____

_____

_____

_____

_____

_____

_____

_____

_____

_____

_____

_____

_____

_____

_____

_____

To spare oneself from grief at all cost can be achieved only at the price of total detachment, which excludes the ability to experience happiness.

Erich Fromm

79. I mourn because I am not detached. I feel my feelings and today as I write I feel:

_____

_____

_____

_____

_____

_____

_____

_____

_____

_____

_____

_____

_____

_____

_____

_____

_____

_____

It is very tempting to want to 'hate' grief,

to see it as the enemy, the unwelcome guest.

Instead, try opening yourself to grief . . .

ask it what it has to teach you.

Ask it what it is training you to do, to be.

Ask this uninvited teacher into your life

and notice how things begin to shift.

Remember that grief never asks you to let go of love.

Ashley Davis Prend

80. Dear Grief, I want to write you a letter.

___ / ___ /

_____

_____

_____

_____

_____

_____

_____

_____

_____

_____

_____

_____

_____

_____

_____

_____

_____

_____

_____

_____

They are not dead who live in lives they leave behind.   In those whom they have blessed, they live again, and shall live through the years eternal life, and shall grow each day more beautiful, as time declares their good, forgets the rest, and proves their immortality.

Hugh Robert Orr

81. A memory I can pass on forever of your beautiful vitality:

/ /

Each of us has his own rhythm of suffering.

Roland Barthes

82. Heck, I just want to feel : miserable a while longer

/ /

_____

_____

_____

_____

_____

_____

_____

_____

_____

_____

_____

_____

_____

_____

_____

_____

_____

_____

Sadness is but a wall between two gardens.

Kahlil Gibran

83. Can I spy a garden, some flowers, nourishing vegetables?

_____

_____

_____

_____

_____

_____

_____

_____

_____

_____

_____

_____

_____

_____

_____

_____

_____

_____

Rain On a Grave

Clouds spout upon her
Their waters amain
In ruthless disdain, --
Her who but lately
Had shivered with pain
As at a touch of dishonor
If there had lit on her
So coldly, so straightly
Such arrows of rain:

One who to shelter
Her delicate head
Would quicken and quicken
Each tentative tread
If drops chanced to pelt her
That summertime spills
In dust—paven rills
When thunder-clouds thicken
And birds close their bills.

Would that I lay there
And she were housed here
Or better, together
Were folded away there
Exposed to one weather
We both, -- who would stray there
When sunny the day there
Or evening was clear
At the prime of the year.

Soon will be growing
Green blades from her mound,
And daisies be showing
Like stars on the ground,
Till she form part of them—
Ay—the sweet heart of them,
Loved beyond measure
With a child's pleasure
All her life's round.

Thomas Hardy

84. Soon will be growing

_____

_____

_____

_____

_____

_____

_____

_____

_____

_____

_____

_____

_____

_____

_____

_____

_____

_____

_____

_____

I wish you enough sun

to keep your attitude bright.

I wish you enough rain

to help you appreciate the sun more.

I wish you enough happiness

to keep your spirit alive.

I wish you enough pain

so that the smallest joys in life

appear much bigger.

I wish you enough gain

to satisfy your wanting.

I wish you enough loss

to appreciate all that you possess.

I wish you enough "hellos"

to get through final "goodbye".

Anonymous

85. Somehow, I had enough time with the one I lost, and I wish for myself enough . . .

_____ / _____ / _____

_____

_____

_____

_____

_____

_____

_____

_____

_____

_____

_____

_____

_____

_____

_____

_____

_____

If you can find a path with no obstacles, it probably doesn't lead anywhere.

Frank A. Clark

86. What path will I take today?   /   /

Time it was - what a time it was.

A time of innocence; a time of confidences.

Long ago, it must be - I have a photograph.

Preserve your memories. They're all that's left you.

Paul Simon ♫

87. A time of innocence. A photograph. A memory.

/ /

Think of a lifeless forest in which a small plant pushes its head upward, out of the ruin. In our grief process, we are moving into life from death, without denying the devastation that came before.

Elisabeth Kübler-Ross

88. A tree, a plant, a step into life: / /

Grief can't be shared. Everyone carries it alone. His own burden in his own way

Anne Morrow Lindbergh

89. What my grief looks like   / /

Though lovers be lost, love shall not;

And death shall have no dominion.

Dylan Thomas

90. Love stays

There are as many nights as days, and the one is just as long as the other in the year's course. Even a happy life cannot be without a measure of darkness, and the word 'happy' would lose its meaning if it were not balanced by sadness.

Carl Jung

91. A balance of happy and sad. I deserve to feel it all.

/   /

_____

_____

_____

_____

_____

_____

_____

_____

_____

_____

_____

_____

_____

_____

_____

_____

_____

_____

She was no longer wresting with the grief, but could sit down with it as a lasting companion and make it a sharer in her thoughts.

George Eliot

92. I am not the same person I was now that I understand loss more deeply than before. How have I grown?

_____

_____

_____

_____

_____

_____

_____

_____

_____

_____

_____

_____

_____

_____

_____

_____

_____

_____

You can clutch the past so tightly to your chest that it leaves your arms too full to embrace the present.

Jan Glidwell

93. Moments, smells and sounds in the present

/ /

_____

_____

_____

_____

_____

_____

_____

_____

_____

_____

_____

_____

_____

_____

_____

_____

_____

_____

_____

_____

_____

_____

When one door of happiness closes, another opens; but often we look so long at the closed door that we do not see the one which has been opened for us.

Helen Keller

94. A door

/ /

The pain passes,
but the beauty remains.

Pierre Auguste Renoir

95. Beauty

/ /

God gave us memories that
we might have roses
in December.

J. M. Barrie

96. A rose

/ /

Good-night! good-night! as we so oft have said

Beneath this roof at midnight, in the days

That are no more, and shall no more return.

Thou hast but taken up thy lamp and gone to bed;

I stay a little longer, as one stays

To cover up the embers that still burn.

Henry Wadsworth Longfellow

97. The embers that still burn / /

One cannot get through life without pain...What we can do is choose how to use the pain life presents to us. -

Bernie S. Siegel

98. What tribute or memorial might I make to honor my loss?

_____

_____

_____

_____

_____

_____

_____

_____

_____

_____

_____

_____

_____

_____

_____

_____

_____

_____

_____

_____

We honor the dead more by
choosing to live well.

Geoff Warburton

99. How might I choose to live well?   / /

_____

_____

_____

_____

_____

_____

_____

_____

_____

_____

_____

_____

_____

_____

_____

_____

_____

_____

_____

There are no goodbyes for us.

Wherever you are, you will always be in my heart.

Mahatma Gandhi

100. Memories of you

Unable are the loved to die.

For love is immortality.

Emily Dickinson

101. What I loved, and now, a real "good-bye"

_____

_____

_____

_____

_____

_____

_____

_____

_____

_____

_____

_____

_____

_____

_____

_____

_____

_____

_____

_____

_____

A few more resources and suggestions

You might be especially comforted from other books or websites directed toward survivors of a parallel loss to yours. As an example and purely by chance I found an old gem of a short hardcover book directed particularly to widows first written in 1988 by 3 widows. It reflects its age, but the ideas are universal. It is called **Beyond Loss: A practical guide through grief to a meaningful life** by Lilly Singer, Margaret Sirot and Susan Rodd and was reprinted in paperback in 2002. I like this book because of its no-nonsense advice and checklists including 20 "points to remember" at the end of each of its chapters on topics such as finance, family, grieving, and moving forward.

I considered appending a bibliography page here, but decided you can google search as easily as I can and I didn't want to include any works I can't truly recommend. I have read a number of personal books on loss including memoirs. Some I liked; some I found repetitive or poorly edited. You can try searches for prenatal loss, parents who've lost children (including some very well-known writers), military families in grief, grieving your parents' deaths, loss of pets, or whatever else you want to find commiseration for including romantic breakup, adjusting to a new location or even expatriate life. There are fabulous resources for parents guiding children through loss and family adjustment. And beautiful children's books have been created for every sort of change a child might have to endure. I found some very nice free files for parents of young children at the Sesame Street source: http://www.pbs.org/parents/whenfamiliesgrieve/

As you can suppose, I love old-fashioned books but of course there are innumerable blogs in which interaction with the blog writer and followers could provide enormous comfort, strength, support and even a sense of community. I also mentioned in the introduction that I have found certain movies, poetry and songs to be cathartic and soothing.

In addition you could search "grief and loss bibliography; pdf" if you want to see what books librarians or academics suggest for example, or go to Amazon, Barnes and Noble and other bookselling sites and see what popular books they have listed for death, bereavement and loss. As a book-lover, I would say go to the public library or nearby large bookstore and engage the staff therein while also physically browsing around the books on bereavement.

Elisabeth Kübler-Ross was the great research psychologist into the grieving process who gave the world the 5-stage paradigm of grieving. The most well-known of her 16+ books are **On Death and Dying** aimed toward medical and psychological professionals and **On Grief and Grieving**, written with David Kessler which will certainly provide you with academic insights into the course of bereavement.

C.S. Lewis the well-known 20th century professor and author of the Chronicles of Narnia and many works of fiction and

Christian theology wrote a journal of his grief and questioning of his religion when his wife died from cancer. **A Grief Observed** is a beautiful short book which opens with the thoughtful sentence I included in this journal.

During the time I was preparing this book, I also looked at my dear friend, youtube, and found a TEDx talk from 2012 in Brighton, England. Psychotherapist Geoff Warburton, whom I quoted above in the journal, delivered an impassioned talk and I transcribed the following (but I suggest you see his moving delivery if you can).

> *Keep your heart open . . . Stay with your experience . . . In grief you're going to meet hate; you're going to meet anger; you're going to meet emotional pain; you're going to meet rage; you're going to meet terror If you get through that you're probably going to feel torn to pieces you might feel crazy you might end up in a total emotional abyss. . . . You need to feel that emotional abyss. You need to let that abyss swallow you . . . . You may feel in that abyss that a part of you is dying. And Maybe a part of you needs to die. Close off your experience of the abyss and you close off the flow of life . . . Block that anger and you block your vitality. Block that fear and you block your excitement. Block that deep emotional pain and you block your access to compassion. Even block your hatred and you'll block your access to peace. Block your experience of that abyss and you will block access to the depths of who you really are and the energy that's going to take you forward. . . . Right in the center of that abyss--in that silence, you will find your liberation.*

I bless you to be liberated and to have pulled yourself out of the abyss of your pain.

Let me also remind you that being alone is an option, not a sentence, no matter how your path wends toward your meaningful life after loss.

I very often choose solitude because I love reading and clicking on my computer. Another person will decide based on a more extroverted personality to be much more occupied and preoccupied with other people or through the necessity of a job. Some aggrieved people avoid being alone with their memories; others find themselves feeling intensely lonely and don't know how to transcend such heartache. Consider and journal about what you can do to alleviate feelings of loneliness or recurrent painful memories.

One specific choice of utter importance to my well-being is to limit the time I spend among negative, energy-draining people including an extended member of my family or two. I'm old enough and adult enough not to be shamed or guilted into the company, beyond the basically polite and unavoidable, of people who drag my emotions down, raise my anger or otherwise too easily test my efforts to remain calm and serene.

Creating impermeable boundaries with a few people has permanently elevated my overall life satisfaction including boosting my sense of self-esteem. I stress this point because family members in the wake of a big shake-up sometimes create dysfunctional alliances. If you are being clung to by someone who is pulling you down or impinging on your ability to flourish, consider family therapy, counseling, or acting on information found in self-help books for assertiveness training or dealing with toxic family systems. Find the words you need to verbalize your own needs for space, time and distance when it's appropriate. Of course, journal writing is a wonderful tool for practice dialogues or drafting letters that don't have to be sent.

A book like this could go on and on as so many writers have written about their own losses and grieving process. I'll end as I began with a quotation. One of the books I liked and quoted from was written by psychotherapist Judy Tatelbaum and first published in 1980. It is **The Courage to Grieve: Creative Living, Recovery and Growth Through Grief**. She wrote at the end of that book,

> *As we journey through these painful experiences of living, we must never forget that we have an amazing resilience and capacity to survive. . . .It takes courage to believe we can survive, that we will grow. It takes courage, too, to live now and not postpone living until some vague tomorrow.*

So I also bless you to develop your resilience and courage and not to postpone your life.

Afterword

Enormous appreciation and acknowledgments go to
Avraham and Daniel, my champions who endure my hours
on computer. I am indebted also to my bereavement
counselors' group, clients who've confided in me and several
dear friends and family members who have helped and
supported me in my publishing endeavors and read my
writings before publication. The creation of this book was
partially and sadly inspired by the unexpected death of my
sister-in-law, Margarette Fried Shafarman at the end of 2012.
I send blessings to her children, my niece and nephew, to
thrive and flourish.

My book of Grief is also lovingly dedicated to the memory
of Rivka Matitya and Zev Friedman.

Many of the quotations and all of the complete poems
included in this journal are in the public domain. If a
copyright infringement appears here or other unintended
error, please write to me and I will promptly modify the book
for future printings.

Thank you all for continuing to encourage the work of
independent professional publishers.

Please take a minute to show your support by posting book
reviews at booksellers' sites on the internet. They are very
well-appreciated and nourish writers who live by words.

.

Judy Shafarman is the creator of New Vision Publications, independent publishing. She has been a teacher for some 3 decades in several countries and nowadays conducts workshops and classes on reflective journal writing and cultivating joy. She writes at judyshafarman.net

Judy Shafarman is the author/compiler of

Journal: 365+ Writing Prompts, Ideas and Quotes to cultivate joy and well-being

> This book contains close to 400 quotes and many ideas about journal keeping, *entirely* different from this collection.

My Book of Appreciation: A Journal

> This book contains 101 quotes and writing prompts to complement and serve as a companion to this book.

Please send your feedback and comments to

judy@Judyshafarman.net

Or

Facebook.com/New-Vision-Publications-Independent-publishing

www.ingramcontent.com/pod-product-compliance
Lightning Source LLC
Chambersburg PA
CBHW032104280326
41933CB00009B/751